S0-BCR-130

HARPER **LEE**

Pulitzer Prize–Winning Author

HARPER **LEE**

Pulitzer Prize–Winning Author

BY ALEXIS BURLING

CONTENT CONSULTANT
R. BARTON PALMER
CALHOUN LEMON PROFESSOR OF LITERATURE
DIRECTOR OF FILM STUDIES
DEPARTMENT OF ENGLISH
CLEMSON UNIVERSITY

Essential Library

An Imprint of Abdo Publishing | abdopublishing.com

abdopublishing.com

Published by Abdo Publishing, a division of ABDO, PO Box 398166, Minneapolis,
Minnesota 55439. Copyright © 2016 by Abdo Consulting Group, Inc. International
copyrights reserved in all countries. No part of this book may be reproduced in any form
without written permission from the publisher. Essential Library™ is a trademark and
logo of Abdo Publishing.

Printed in the United States of America, North Mankato, Minnesota
062015
092015

Cover Photo: AP Images
Interior Photos: AP Images, 2, 9; Hulton Archive/Getty Images, 6; World History
Archive/Newscom, 11; Richard B. Levine/Newscom, 14; Charlie Varley/Sipa USA/
Newscom, 16, 61; John Lent/AP Images, 22; Bettmann/Corbis, 26; Arnold Genthe/
Library of Congress, 31; Rob Carr/AP Images, 33; Cliff Welch/Icon SMI 357/Cliff
Welch/Icon SMI /Newscom, 36; Donald Uhrbrock/The LIFE Images Collection/Getty
Images, 40, 55, 74; Henry Griffin/AP Images, 43; William Straeter/AP Images, 46;
Lee Celano/WireImage/Getty Images, 48; Thomas Cordy/ZumaPress/Newscom, 51;
Universal Pictures/Album/Newscom, 58; PF1 WENN Photos/Newscom, 62; Corbis/
Splash News/Newscom, 68; Keystone Pictures USA/ZumaPress/Newscom, 70; Carl
T. Gossett Jr./New York Times Co./Getty Images, 79; Jamie Martin/AP Images, 81;
Terrence Antonio James/KRT/Newscom, 82; Gerald Herbert/AP Images, 85; Teresa
Crawford/AP Images, 88; Stringer/Reuters/Corbis, 91; Gary Tramontina/Polaris/
Newscom, 95

Editor: Mirella Miller
Series Designer: Becky Daum

Library of Congress Control Number: 2015934083

Cataloging-in-Publication Data

Burling, Alexis.
 Harper Lee: Pulitzer Prize-winning author / Alexis Burling.
  p. cm. -- (Essential lives)
Includes bibliographical references and index.
ISBN 978-1-62403-894-5
1. Lee, Harper--Juvenile literature. 2. Authors, American--20th century--Biography--
Juvenile literature. I. Title.
813/.54--dc23
[B]   2015934083

CONTENTS

CHAPTER
ONE

ENOUGH!

It was the dead of winter in New York City in 1958, and Nelle Harper Lee was busy revising the manuscript of her first novel. The 32-year-old had not taken a walk or eaten much of anything in days. Her cramped apartment on York Avenue on Manhattan's Upper East Side was freezing, the crisp outside air making temperatures inside virtually intolerable. But Lee would not let her chattering teeth or her grumbling stomach bother her. She had work to do.

Lee threaded another blank page into her typewriter. In what had become a daily routine, she stayed up late and woke up with the sun, writing and reworking her manuscript. The work was difficult. Lee was on yet another draft. There seemed to be no end in sight.

Atticus

For two years, Lee had been working with her agent on a novel she originally planned to call *Go Set a Watchman*. The book, later called *Atticus*, and eventually *To Kill*

A young Harper Lee smiles for her portrait in 1960, the year her first published novel became a success.

a Mockingbird, was about a woman named Jean Louise "Scout" Finch, who returns home to Alabama after years of living in New York in order to reconnect with her roots. When Lee submitted an early draft of the manuscript to her publisher, her editor suggested Lee try telling the story from a different perspective. "My editor, who was taken by the flashbacks to Scout's childhood, persuaded me to write [another] novel . . . from the point of view of the young Scout," Lee later explained. "I was a first-time writer, so I did as I was told."[1]

Loosely based on actual events from Lee's childhood, *Atticus*'s plot revolved around a white man named Atticus Finch who lived with his family in a fictional town called Maycomb, Alabama,

Atticus Finch in the movie adaptation of *To Kill a Mockingbird*

during the 1930s. Similar to Lee's father, Atticus was a well-respected lawyer, and many of Maycomb's townsfolk looked to him to make important decisions. But when he agreed to represent an African-American man named Tom Robinson who was accused of raping a white woman, many of those same supporters turned their backs on Atticus and his family.

The circumstances of Robinson's case were grounded in truth. During the 1930s, the United States was involved in a race war that showed no sign of stopping. Especially in southern states such as Alabama, African Americans and whites were not seen as equals. In fact, many whites viewed African Americans as inferior. Schools were segregated. Many African Americans had a difficult time finding steady employment and could not vote. The Ku Klux Klan lynched innocent African Americans

Lee's work focused on racial issues that were prominent in the United States during the 1930s.

and placed burning crosses in the yards of any white person associated with them. Having grown up in the Deep South, Lee wanted the world to know about the entrenched problems the South was facing. A book such as *Atticus* was the perfect way to spread the word.

Atticus also served another purpose—it described a racially divided United States as seen through the eyes of an innocent, imaginative, and highly impressionable young girl. The story's young narrator, Scout Finch, closely resembled Lee as a child—tomboyish, big-hearted, and insatiably curious. Much of the mischief

Scout, her brother, Jem, and their next-door neighbor and friend Dill Harris got involved in mirrored some of the pranks Lee pulled during her childhood, including sneaking around an old house rumored to be inhabited by a hermit. This hermit would eventually become the inspiration for one of literature's most enduring and fascinating characters, Boo Radley.

> "I like to write. Sometimes I'm afraid that I like it too much because when I get into work I don't want to leave it. As a result I'll go for days and days without leaving the house or wherever I happen to be. I'll go out long enough to get papers and pick up some food and that's it. It's strange, but instead of hating writing I love it too much."[3]
>
> —Harper Lee, speaking to Roy Newquist in an interview on WQXR radio

Frustration Wins Out

In Lee's mind, *Atticus* was still many months away from completion. She had already discarded the first draft, which was written in the third person. She then started working on a second draft, which she tried writing in first person. And despite constant reassurance from her editor, Tay Hohoff, Lee still was not sure that the latest draft, written in both past and present tense and using flashbacks, made any sense.

Lee looked over at the page that was threaded into the typewriter. Then she read it again for the third time. Suddenly, in a fit of frustration, she ripped out the page, gathered up the rest of the papers scattered around the floor next to her desk, briskly opened the window, and chucked the entire pile decisively into the New York night.

Looking down, Lee watched in horror as her life's work fluttered into the alley behind her apartment and onto the snow-covered city streets below. What had she done? Was her book really so awful? After years of struggle, everything she had worked so hard to produce was being carried away by the wind! What could be worth throwing all of it away?

Saved

Full of regret, Lee picked up the phone and dialed Hohoff. She explained her foolish panic attack and its disastrous consequences. After calming Lee down, Hohoff demanded that she march downstairs to retrieve the manuscript immediately. She had worked too hard to succumb to self-doubt now, Hohoff said. The story just needed a little more finessing.

To Kill a Mockingbird would have several reprints after 1960,
some of which came with new book jacket designs.

Once again, Lee realized it was best to follow her editor's orders. After recovering what could be salvaged, she got back to work. "I knew I could never be happy being anything but a writer. . . . I kept at it because I knew it had to be my first novel, for better or for worse."[4]

Over the next few weeks and months, Hohoff helped Lee put the finishing touches on her story, including changing the name of the book from *Atticus* to *To Kill a Mockingbird*. By the time the spring of 1959 rolled around, the manuscript was in perfect shape. When it was published in July 1960, Lee was pleased by how it had turned out. Little did she know it would come to be regarded as one of the greatest works of literature the world had ever seen.

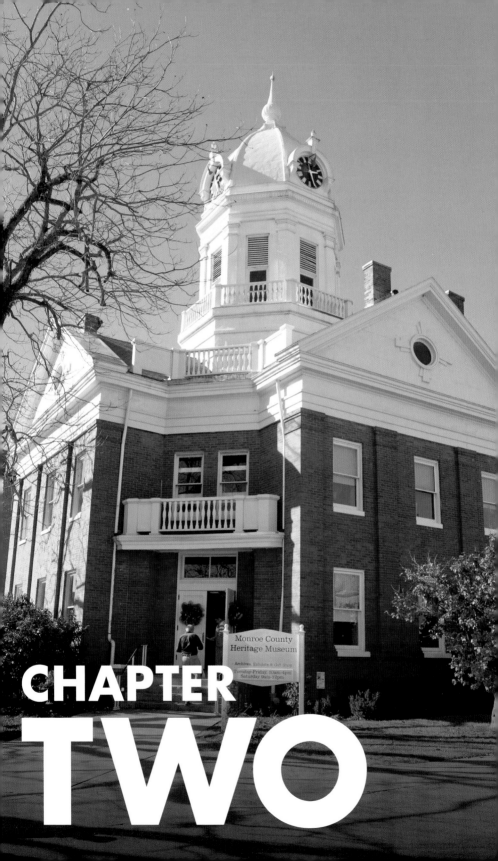

CHAPTER
TWO

MONROEVILLE

Nelle Harper Lee was born on April 28, 1926, in Monroeville, Alabama. She was the youngest of four children—two sisters and an older brother. Alice, 15 years Nelle's senior and the oldest child in the Lee family, was smart and studious, while middle sister Louise was known as the pretty one. Nelle's brother, Edwin, was six years old when Nelle was born, and the two were extremely close.

Because she lived in the South, Nelle's upbringing was full of "yes, ma'am" and "no, sir." Her father, Amasa Coleman Lee, who was often called AC for short, was one of the most respected men in Monroeville. Though he was born in Alabama in 1880, he spent his childhood tilling a farm in rural Florida, listening to sermons in the local church every Sunday, and minding his manners. When he was 16, AC became a teacher and earned his keep until he moved back to Alabama at 19 to take a job as a bookkeeper for a mill.

Growing up in Monroeville, Alabama, would serve as inspiration for Nelle's future novel.

AC was a hard worker and strove to move up in the world. Before long, and a few increasingly better jobs later, he settled in a town called Finchburg in 1905, where he met his future wife, Frances Cunningham Finch. Frances had grown up on a sprawling 9,000-acre (3,640 ha) plantation and was highly educated and refined, spending her days reading, playing piano, and politely flirting with the handsome young man named AC whom she had met at church. When she was 19 years old and AC was 30, the two married, on June 22, 1910. One year later, Frances gave birth to their first child, Alice.

A Lucky Move

At the end of 1912, the Lee family relocated to Monroeville, which had a population of 750 people. AC accepted a prestigious position as the finance manager of the Bugg & Barnett law firm, and it could not have been at a better time. The freshly laid tracks of the Manistee & Repton Railroad had just been completed. With the arrival of trains came commerce and people. Monroeville's drafty wooden municipal buildings were replaced with sturdier brick constructions. New retail stores and a rebuilt courthouse joined the old cotton gin, fertilizer plant, lumber mill, and sawmill. A larger county high school was built to accommodate the influx of children whose parents had come to the area seeking employment.

For nearly two decades, the Lees continued to flourish. After they moved into a white house with a picket fence and a porch swing on South Alabama Avenue, their family nearly doubled in size as Louise and Edwin were born in 1916 and 1920, respectively. When Nelle arrived in 1926, AC had already passed the bar

OLD MONROEVILLE

Similar to many old southern towns, Monroeville has a rich and interesting history. A pioneer named Major Walker first settled the area in the early 1800s. Poor cotton farmers and employees of the lumber mill lived in Monroeville after the American Civil War (1861–1865) ended. When the Manistee & Repton Railroad arrived in 1912, connecting Monroeville to bigger cities such as Selma, Alabama, and Pensacola, Florida, circumstances improved, bringing people, jobs, and commerce. Little by little, modern conveniences started appearing. Electricity and running water arrived in 1923. In 1928, the first airport was built. In 1930, a working sewage system was installed. Eight years later, Monroeville boasted its first traffic light. Though still small by today's standards, with a population nearing 6,500, contemporary Monroeville is a bustling town full of cafés, shopping malls, and municipal buildings.[1] Though many buildings are new, the Monroe County Courthouse is still standing and now operates as a museum.

exam and become an attorney, changing the name of the company he worked for from Bugg & Barnett to Barnett, Bugg & Lee. Not to be outdone by his own determination to succeed, he was also a proud member of the Alabama State legislature, and in 1929, he became the editor and publisher of the *Monroe Journal*, a job he would hold until 1947.

But though AC was thriving in his professional life, something seemed to be wrong at home. The Wall Street stock market crash of 1929 and the ensuing Great Depression meant money was tight not just for the Lees and people in Monroeville, but across the country. Many people became unemployed, and new jobs were hard to find. Prices for common goods such as grains, produce, and gas skyrocketed.

Frances had also grown increasingly depressed since her children were born. She suffered through mood swings and barely set foot outside. The cleaning and most of the cooking were, instead, taken care of daily by an African-American housekeeper. Marie Faulk Rudisill, a neighbor, remembered Frances in an interview:

> We went to Mrs. Lee's practically every day. She was very kind . . . [but] she didn't talk to us at all. I never saw her even speak to one of her children. She got up in the morning and started playing that darned piano all day long . . . but as far as providing companionship for the children that wasn't so because Mrs. Lee never left the house.[2]

By the time Nelle was five years old, steering clear of her mother had become routine. Instead, Nelle preferred climbing trees, reading books, or enjoying the company of her father or brother. Luckily, a new visitor came to town in 1930 who effectively turned her friendless world upside down.

Truman Streckfus Persons

From the moment Nelle laid eyes on almost six-year-old Truman Streckfus Persons, she knew they would get along famously. Truman had just moved in next door with his elderly, unmarried relatives. He was exceedingly pale and slightly feminine. His flamboyant clothes were a bit too hoity-toity for his small frame, and

Truman and Nelle would stay close friends throughout much of their lives.

the rest of the kids in the neighborhood and at school called him a sissy. But never one to care what anyone else thought, the tomboyish Nelle overlooked Truman's eccentricities, and the two soon became fast friends.

"Nelle was too rough for the girls, and Truman was scared of the boys, so he just tagged on to her and she was his protector," recalled Charles Ray Skinner, a childhood friend of Edwin Lee.[3]

For the next few years, Truman was the ideal playmate for Nelle. They rode their bikes down to the drugstore where they could get soda fountain drinks for a nickel. They devoured book series such as the Rover Boys and Sherlock Holmes in Nelle's tree house and spied on the old house down the street that belonged to a crazy old man and his mysterious son. And they invented outlandish tales, typing up scripts and

THE REAL BOO RADLEY

Boo Radley is one of the spookiest characters in literature. But he is also based on a real boy who lived down the street from Nelle during her childhood. According to local legend, Alfred "Son" Boleware was caught breaking into a store with his friends. As a punishment, the other boys were sent to reform school. But instead of sending Sonny away, his father locked him up in their dilapidated house. Son lived that way for most of his life, rarely venturing out. From that day forward, the neighborhood kids made up fantastical, often ghoulish stories about his fate.

stories on the black Underwood No. 5 typewriter Nelle's father had given her as a present in elementary school. As Nelle recalled in an interview with author Roy Newquist years later,

> If I went to a film once a month it was pretty good for me, and for all children like me. We had to use our own devices in our play, for our entertainment. We didn't have much money. Nobody had any money. We didn't have toys, nothing was done for us, so the result was that we lived in our imagination most of the time. We devised things; we were readers, and we would transfer everything we had seen on the printed page to the backyard in the form of high drama.[4]

Nelle also had a temper. Thanks to her fearless attitude and because Truman was teased so mercilessly, she often became entangled in brawls at school. On one occasion, Nelle took on three boys at once. The group's ringleader had yanked Nelle's hair one time too many, and she refused to let him get away with it. "In my mind's eye I can still see the fire in those big brown eyes as they stared dead ahead," a schoolmate of Nelle's named George Thomas Jones told the *Monroe Journal* about the incident. "Her teeth clenched in jaws set as only could be akin to a full-blood bulldog. Her tiny hands balled into tight firsts as she strode defiantly from the playground back toward her fourth-grade classroom."[5]

Despite her aggressive behavior and his obvious sensitivities, Nelle and Truman were inseparable. Though Truman moved to New York City in 1933 to live with his mother and her second husband, Joseph Capote, he returned to Monroeville every summer to spend time with Nelle. The friendship they forged during those childhood years would last well into adulthood. And the experiences they shared in Monroeville would inspire the careers of what would soon become two of the greatest writers in US history.

TRUMAN'S TROUBLED BACKGROUND

Throughout his life, Truman Capote (who changed his last name from Persons to Capote when his mother got remarried) was known for being eccentric, needy, and weird. Some say that was just his personality. But others attribute it partly to Truman's troubled childhood. Truman and his mother, Lillie Mae, left Truman's birth father, Arch Persons, early on. Truman's stepfather, Joe Capote, served a year in prison for embezzling money from his own company. And Lillie Mae was a depressed alcoholic who criticized Truman for his homosexuality and flamboyant nature. She committed suicide in 1954.

CHAPTER
THREE

A WRITER EMERGES

B y the time Lee graduated Monroe County High School in 1944, she was ready for something—and someplace—new. Following in her sister Alice's footsteps, she attended Huntingdon College in Montgomery, Alabama. With her white Bermuda shorts, unkempt hair and lack of makeup, new pipe-smoking habit, colorful vocabulary, and continued refusal to conform to anyone's notion of how a lady should act, Lee did not exactly fit in with the rest of the students.

As Catherine Helms, a classmate of Lee's remembered:

> I didn't have anything in common with her because she was not like most of us. . . . She wasn't worried about how her hair looked or whether she had a date on Friday night like the rest of us were. I don't remember her sitting around and giggling and being silly and talking about what our weddings were going to be like—that's what teenage girls talked about. She was not part of the girl group.[1]

Lee had different habits and more grown-up interests than many of her female classmates in high school and college.

Lee's studies and extracurricular activities at Huntingdon did not satisfy her appetite either. Lee belonged to a singing group, got excellent grades, and was inducted into the campus's chapter of a literary honor society, Chi Delta Phi. She also wrote two short stories for the college's *Prelude* literary magazine, but decided to transfer to the University of Alabama in Tuscaloosa in 1945, after her freshman year. Her plan was to study law and join Barnett, Bugg & Lee when she completed her degree, just as Alice had done.

At the start of her junior year in 1946, Lee applied to the University of Alabama's law school and was accepted. Perhaps for reasons fully unbeknownst to her at the time, she also started spending more time working on pieces for *Rammer Jammer*, the university's humor magazine, and writing snarky updates about college life or the latest cultural trends for

A WINK AT JUSTICE—AND AT FATE

When it was published, Lee's *To Kill a Mockingbird* was a huge success. But over the years, a number of smaller works of hers were also in print, including essays for *O* magazine, *McCall's*, and *Vogue*. Her first short stories, "A Wink at Justice" and "Nightmare," were both courtroom dramas and ran in the 1945 spring edition of the Huntingdon College literary magazine, the *Prelude*.

Caustic Comment, her weekly column for the campus newspaper, the *Crimson White*. When she was appointed editor in chief of the *Rammer Jammer* that same year, her taste for writing politically relevant stories was cemented firmly into place.

Due to her heavy workload for law school and because managing an editorial staff came with perhaps too much responsibility, Lee lasted as editor in chief for only one year. But the experience of writing every day and thinking about words was enough to throw significant doubt onto what was, up to that point, a solid plan to practice law. When AC offered to send her to Oxford University in England for a summer, hoping to persuade his daughter to choose law as a profession so she could afford to continue writing on the side, the scheme backfired. After

UNDERGRADUATE LAW DEGREE

These days most students who wish to become lawyers have to apply to law school after they finish their undergraduate degree. But when Lee was in college, that was not always the case. At the time Lee was attending the University of Alabama, interested students could apply to the school's law program as juniors. The only requirement was at least a C average in all of their classes. Lee eagerly took advantage of the opportunity. Still, she found it difficult. Aside from the grueling schedule on top of the rest of her studies, most prelaw students were men.

only a few weeks studying the works of literary giants such as Virginia Woolf and T. S. Eliot, Lee was smitten with the idea of becoming an author herself. When she returned home to Alabama, she abandoned her studies altogether and dropped out of school just a few months shy of graduating with neither a law degree nor an undergraduate diploma to her name.

In the spring of 1949, Lee returned home to Monroeville. But she did not mope around the house. Instead, the 23-year-old packed up her belongings and headed off to find Truman. Lee moved to New York City to pursue a career as a writer.

A Rocky Start

From the moment Lee arrived in New York City in 1949, the tall buildings, the loud honking of cars and buses, and the variety of clothing stores and restaurants

The hustle and bustle of New York City was a
big change from Monroeville for Lee.

open at all hours overwhelmed her. Life was so different
from the small-town Alabama she was used to. Unlike
the South, which was still mostly segregated, New York
City was filled with people of all racial backgrounds.
And it was overflowing with vibrant culture and
art—exactly where a blossoming writer should be when
working on a novel.

Lee found an apartment on the Upper East Side
of Manhattan at 1539 York Avenue, two blocks from
the East River. It was tiny and did not have hot water.
But it would serve her simple, quiet lifestyle just fine.

Lee cycled through a series of low-paying jobs before settling into a position as an airplane reservations agent, first for Eastern Airlines and then for the British Overseas Airways Corporation. The job did not have anything to do with her aspirations, but it helped pay the bills.

When Lee was not at work or revising rough drafts of stories, she was often hanging out with Capote and his gaggle of artsy friends. Capote was already well on his way to becoming a successful author, with short stories in *Harper's Bazaar* and *Mademoiselle*, a semi-autobiographical novel entitled *Other Voices, Other Rooms* published in 1948, and a book based on his childhood called *The Grass Harp* on the way. Almost as if their situations were now reversed, Capote became Lee's protector, introducing her to agents, editors, and other artists in hopes of spurring her career as a writer.

But just as Lee was getting into the swing of life in New York City, tragedy struck back home. On June 2, 1951, Lee's mother, Frances, died after being ill for many months. Six weeks later, on July 12, Lee's 30-year-old brother, Edwin, died of a sudden brain hemorrhage, leaving behind his widow, Sara, their three-year-old daughter, Mary, and nine-month-old

Lee got right back to work after tragedy struck her family.

son, Edwin Jr. Lee was devastated by the loss of her brother, yet it did not stop her from heading back to her apartment in New York once funeral services had concluded.

Merry Christmas, Lee

For the next five years, Lee spent nearly all of her free time writing. By 1956, she had cobbled together a series of short stories to submit to a literary agent, hoping he or she could then sell them to a publisher. On the recommendation of a friend of Capote's named Michael Brown, Lee submitted her work to agent Annie Laurie Williams just after Thanksgiving.

"I walked around the block three times before I could muster the courage to go in and give the stories to the agent," Lee told a reporter for the *Delta Review* years later. "At the time, I was very shy. Finally, I rushed in, left the manuscripts with the secretary, and left. I prayed for a quick death, and forgot about it."[2]

Williams's husband, Maurice Crain, who ended up taking Lee on as a client, rejected most of the stories. But he did politely suggest that Lee should, perhaps, begin work on a novel, which might be easier to sell. The thought of finishing an entire novel was daunting for Lee. Where would she find the energy with a full-time job? But a few weeks later, a surprise Christmas present from Brown and his wife, Joy Williams, made the task much more attractive and possible: a check worth enough money that Lee could quit her job and concentrate on writing for one year, no strings attached. Lee recalled that Christmas Day experience in an article for *McCall's* magazine in December 1961:

"It took some time to find my voice," Lee wrote of that Christmas day. "When I did, I asked [Brown and Williams] if they were out of their minds. What made them think anything would come of this? They didn't have that kind of money to throw away. A year was a long time. . . . A full, fair chance for a new life. Not given me by an act of generosity, but by an act of love. Our faith in you was really all I had heard them say."[3]

After a bit more thought, Lee accepted the money and promised she would do her best. With the money in the bank, it was time to get down to business.

AN AMAZING GIFT

Joy Williams and Michael Brown were influential figures in Lee's life. Williams was a former ballerina. Brown was a cabaret singer and Broadway lyricist who also wrote motivational party jingles for companies such as J.C. Penney and Singer sewing machines. The husband-and-wife pair did not have a lot of money, but they were flush when Brown had a successful year. When Lee first arrived in New York in 1949, Capote sent Brown a letter. A friend of his was coming to the city, and he wanted them to look after her. Always generous people, Brown and Williams were happy to do so. During Christmas in 1956, Lee could not afford to make the trip home to Monroeville.

CHAPTER FOUR

ATTICUS TAKES SHAPE

I t was a typical New York spring in 1957, and Lee had been working for months with her agent, Maurice Crain, on a manuscript originally titled *Go Set a Watchman,* and later *Atticus,* when she received promising news. J. B. Lippincott, a prominent book publisher at the time, was interested in Lee's writing. They hoped to set up an in-person meeting to discuss their reaction to her work.

Editor Tay Hohoff remembered her first impression of Lee clearly. "On a hot day in June, a dark-haired, dark-eyed young woman walked shyly into our office on Fifth Avenue to meet most of our editorial staff," she recalled. "They were all men, except me, and apparently we looked formidable. [Lee] has since admitted she was terrified."[1]

As first meetings with editors go, Lee's experience with Hohoff and her team was fairly common. Although

Lee spent much of her late 20s and early 30s perfecting her manuscript with the help of her agent, Maurice Crain.

GETTING PUBLISHED

In Lee's day, the process of getting a book published was much the same as it is today. First, a prospective author wrote part or all of a manuscript. Then, he or she sent a pitch letter to prospective agents who could help find a publisher. Once an agent signed on to the project, he or she could help sell the book to a publisher. When a publisher took over, it usually took one year or more for the book to appear on bookstore shelves. Neither agents nor publishers accepted every book they received. Many manuscripts wound up in the trash. Lee was lucky she found an agent and a publisher on her first try.

they did not offer her a book contract, they did recommend a few helpful pointers on how she might make the manuscript better if she chose to resubmit it at a later date. The chapters were too choppy. The characters were three-dimensional but needed even more depth. And the book's structure needed to be overhauled—her submission read more like a series of short stories than a novel that flowed seamlessly from one end to the other.

Lee took their suggestions to heart, and by the end of the summer she had another draft of *Atticus* ready to show Hohoff. "It was better. It wasn't *right*," Hohoff said. "There were dangling threads of plot, there was a lack of unity—a beginning, a middle, an end that was inherent in the beginning."[2] Plus, Hohoff thought the entire book might be better if it unfolded during Scout's childhood and was told from her perspective. But the manuscript's faults were not enough to deter Hohoff from offering Lee a contract and a few thousand dollars in advance payment. Besides, Lee's willingness to accept criticism meant Hohoff could help her whip the manuscript into publishable shape—sooner rather than later, she hoped.

To Kill a Mockingbird Is Born

For Lee, the next two and a half years were fairly solitary. Occasionally she would take a break and visit the Metropolitan Museum of Art to see an exhibit. But from the end of 1957 through most of 1959, Lee did almost nothing but write. Alternating her time in New York with sporadic months spent in Monroeville with her family or at Capote's aunt Mary Ida Carter's farmhouse in the countryside two miles (3.2 km) outside of Monroeville, she worked on *Atticus* until a cohesive story line emerged.

Though Lee has never admitted as much in the few interviews she took part in, Lee experts and Monroeville

LET'S GO, METS!

Working on *To Kill a Mockingbird* had been a slow-going process for Lee. Like many writers, she loved to procrastinate. When she was in New York City, one of her favorite methods was to go see a baseball game. She liked the Mets more than the Yankees.

It took years for Lee to complete her manuscript.

inhabitants suggest her novel was based partly on a case
she witnessed as a child when her father was editor
of the *Monroe Journal*. On November 9, 1933, a poor,
married white woman named Naomi Lowery told the
police an African-American man named Walter Lett
had raped her outside a factory. According to the paper
(and using the common slang of the time to describe
an African American), Lett was "taken into custody.
Fearing that an attempt would be made to lynch the
Negro by a mob following the news of the attack,

Sheriff Sawyer took the Negro to the jail in Greenville for safekeeping."[3] Six months later, Lett was declared guilty at the Monroe County Courthouse and given the death penalty. Though his sentence was later reduced to life imprisonment thanks to a number of townsfolk, including Lee's father, who suspected Lett was innocent, the damage had already been done. Lett suffered a nervous breakdown and died of tuberculosis in a mental institution in 1937.

Fictionalizing the circumstances of Lett's case and bookending them with versions of stories of her and Capote's adventures during her adolescence, Lee created a snapshot of small-town life in the Deep South just after the Great Depression. The Lett trial became Atticus's defense of Tom Robinson. Lee and Capote morphed into Scout and Dill. And the kids' obsession with the neighborhood bogeyman, Alfred "Son" Boleware, paved the way for the infamous Boo Radley.

"After a couple of false starts, the story line, interplay of characters, and fall of emphasis grew clearer," recalled Hohoff. "With each revision—there were many minor changes as the story grew in strength and in Nelle's own vision of it—the true stature of the novel became evident."[4]

By the fall of 1959, two years after she started writing in earnest, Lee had completed the final draft of *Atticus*—which had been officially renamed *To Kill a Mockingbird*. And Lee was anxiously awaiting the arrival of advance copies all authors receive prior to the publication of their book. But just as she was about to finally take time off from writing, she received an urgent phone call from Capote. The *New Yorker* magazine had hired him to cover a quadruple murder that had taken place in a small town in Kansas. He needed a research assistant to help him conduct interviews, and his old childhood friend was just the person he had in mind.

Two weeks shy of Christmas in 1959, Lee packed her bags once again and hopped on a train to join Capote in Kansas. "He said it would be a tremendously involved job and would take two people," she said. "The crime intrigued him, and I'm intrigued with crime—and, boy, I wanted to go."[5]

Capote called on his good friend Lee to help research
the deaths of the Clutter family in Kansas.

In Cold Blood

On November 16, 1959, a shocking story ran in the
New York Times. A rich farmer, his wife, and two teenage
children, the Clutter family, had been brutally shot
to death by unknown assailants in Holcomb, Kansas.
Nothing had been taken from inside the Clutters'
home where the murders took place, and the telephone
wires had been snipped. "This is apparently the case
of a psychopathic killer," Sheriff Earl Robinson told a
reporter from the paper.[6]

When Lee and Capote arrived in the small Kansas
town, population 270, in mid-December, Holcomb's

THE SCOTTSBORO BOYS TRIAL, 1931–1937

The Scottsboro boys were nine teenage African Americans who were accused of raping two white girls on a Southern Railroad freight train in Alabama on March 25, 1931. In their trial, eight of the boys were given the death penalty. The youngest boy, only 13 at the time, received life in prison. In a series of subsequent trials, four of the boys were released after charges against them were dropped. The others were eventually paroled, except one, who was tried again and sentenced to death. The Scottsboro Trials are also commonly believed to have informed the plot of *To Kill a Mockingbird*.

inhabitants were still reeling from the news. After meeting with Kansas Bureau of Investigation (KBI) detective Alvin Dewey and getting the lay of the land, Lee and Capote planned to interview everyone they could find who might be somehow connected to the slain family. The problem was that the townspeople had already grown tired of reporters swarming their usually sleepy streets, and no one would talk to Capote, especially since he refused to carry press credentials. His sheepskin coat and scarf that trailed past his knees were too fancy. His voice sounded too high-pitched.

People did not trust him. "Capote came walking around here real uppity and superior-like and acting so strange that I think people was scared of him," postmistress Myrtle T. Clare told the *Chicago Sunday Tribune*. "He was real foreign-like, and nobody would open their doors for him, afraid he'd knock them in the head."[7]

But Lee was a different story. She was a straight talker and seemed to put those she was interviewing at ease. People flocked to her—especially KBI detective Dewey and his wife. After a particularly warm dinner party held at the Dewey's over Christmas, Dewey supposedly started to leak more information to Lee and, by default, Capote, than he shared with other reporters. "Nelle got out there and laid some foundations with people. She worked her way around and finally got some contacts with the locals and was able to bring Truman in," said KBI detective Harold Nye.[8]

After Richard Hickock and Perry Smith, two previously convicted felons, were arrested in Las Vegas, Nevada, on December 30, 1959, they both eventually confessed to killing the Clutter family. While in jail a few months earlier, they had heard a rumor from a cellmate about a safe filled with money on the Clutters' farm. On the night of the intended robbery, they slaughtered the family even though the money was nowhere to be found.

With the murder basically solved, Lee and Capote hailed a train back to New York on January 16, 1960,

Police take Perry Smith into custody.

their suitcases stuffed with reams of typewritten notes about the case. When the initial trial date was set for two months later, the two returned to see a verdict delivered. On March 29, 1960, Hickock and Smith were sentenced to death by hanging. Capote now had his story for the *New Yorker* and what would later become the book *In Cold Blood*. Truman's embellished retelling of the circumstances surrounding the Clutter murders was a huge success. None of it would have been possible without the help of Lee.

IN COLD BLOOD CONTROVERSY

Capote's *In Cold Blood* was a huge hit and often considered by scholars as one of the first narrative nonfiction novels to be published—using elements of fiction to tell a mostly factual story. But Capote also received a lot of criticism for how much he stretched the facts of the case in favor of telling a good story. Some sources say the conversations he quoted never happened. Others insist he embellished the truth to sell more copies of his book.

A particular problem arose surrounding Dewey's role in the investigation. In Capote's book, Dewey is a hero. But recent findings suggest he may not have followed up on evidence quickly enough, and the delay allowed Hickock and Smith to continue their murdering spree before they were arrested. It is true that Capote rarely used a tape recorder during his interviews, preferring to record his impressions after his subject had left the room. Perhaps this was Capote's way of making his subjects feel comfortable. Or it may have been an excuse to manufacture details that would tell the best story.

CHAPTER
FIVE

MOCKINGBIRD PUBLISHED

"On July 11th, Lippincott is publishing a delightful book: *To Kill a Mockingbird* . . . Get it. It's going to be a great success," wrote Capote in a letter to his Hollywood friends in 1960. "In it, I am the character called 'Dill'—the author being a childhood friend."[1]

The author Capote was referring to, of course, was 34-year-old Lee. On the eve of *Mockingbird*'s publication, Lee's agent, Crain, and his wife, Williams, threw the soon-to-be-published writer a celebration party. There was a cake frosted to resemble the novel's jacket cover. Champagne and conversation flowed throughout the evening.

It must have come as a relief to see her first big project finally come to fruition. But Lee never predicted it would garner her any lasting attention. Instead she thought "The Bird," as she sometimes called it, would

In 1960, Lee had no idea how much her life would change with the release of her first novel.

make a tiny splash before being forgotten in a sea of other literary novels published at the time—books by already famous authors such as John Updike, Philip Roth, Sylvia Plath, and Jack Kerouac. If she were lucky, perhaps it would open the door to writing another novel.

"I never expected any sort of success with *Mockingbird*," Lee told journalist Roy Newquist, looking back on the book's publication four years later. "I didn't expect the book to sell in the first place. I was hoping for a quick and merciful death at the hands of reviewers, but at the same time I sort of hoped that maybe someone would like it enough to give me encouragement. Public encouragement."[2]

Success Overnight

When a meager print run of 5,000 copies of *To Kill a Mockingbird* was released on July 11, 1960, Lee received far more than mere public encouragement.[3] In fact, over the next few weeks, critics raved about the book's far-reaching appeal. The *Chicago Tribune* called it "an engrossing first novel of rare excellence."[4] The *New York Times* said Lee wrote with "gentle affection, rich humor and deep understanding of small-town family life in Alabama."[5] And the *Washington Post* declared

Lee's book had almost immediate success and praise.

that "[a] hundred pounds of sermons on tolerance, or an equal measure of invective deploring the lack of it, will weigh far less in the scale of enlightenment than a mere 18 ounces of new fiction bearing the title *To Kill a Mockingbird*."[6]

By August, Lee's novel had become a Literary Guild and Book-of-the-Month selection and made both the coveted *New York Times* and the *Chicago Tribune* best seller lists—all rare feats for any first-time author. A larger printing was ordered, and by September, *To Kill a Mockingbird* was flying off bookstore shelves. In the dawn of the civil rights era as demonstrations against prejudice became more commonplace and mentions of riots made daily appearances in front-page news columns, customers nationwide could not wait to get their hands on the book that so aptly described racial injustice and its effects on a small southern community. Readers sent Lee and her publisher letter after letter full of praise about the book to prove it.

"Poor thing—she is nearly demented: says she gave up trying to answer her 'fan mail' when she recieved [sic] 62 letters in one day," Capote wrote to their old friends, KBI detective Dewey and his wife, Marie. "I wish she could relax and enjoy it more."[7]

Yet despite its immense popularity, *Mockingbird* was not read and enjoyed by everyone across the board. Some thought Lee treated the South and its entrenched traditions too harshly. Others, including many African Americans, disliked the idea of a white woman acting as a spokesperson for African Americans' experiences. They felt the story was far too one-dimensional and the prejudice Tom Robinson encountered was too real. Civil rights leader Andrew Young said,

Not a lot of black people read the book. I didn't need to read that. I knew what they were talking about . . . I had been through that with my wife. I had been through that with my father and my grandfather. I remember Emmett Till and all of that drama around that. I was part of the march around Jimmie Lee Jackson's death and the three civil rights workers, James Chaney, Andrew Goodman, and Michael Schwerner. There was too much horror around me at the time for me to absorb more.[8]

Still, by the time winter rolled around, Lee was up to her eyeballs in media interview requests. Already a

THE CIVIL RIGHTS ERA: VOLATILE TIMES

When *To Kill a Mockingbird* was released in 1960, strife was in the air. The fight against prejudice and racial intolerance had reached a pinnacle, and a number of events that took place during those years helped shape the course of history. These are just three of many atrocities that took place:

- On August 28, 1955, 14-year-old Emmett Till was murdered in Mississippi after purportedly flirting with 21-year-old Carolyn Bryant, a white woman. Bryant's husband, Roy, and Roy's half-brother beat Till and gouged out his eyes before shooting him.

- In June 1964, James Chaney, Andrew Goodman, and Michael Schwerner—civil rights workers (two white and one African American)—were shot in Neshoba County, Mississippi. The men were helping get African Americans registered to vote.

- On February 18, 1965, a white state trooper in Marion, Alabama, shot Jimmie Lee Jackson after Jackson participated in a nonviolent protest march. He was shot while protecting his mother and 82-year-old grandmother.

> "It's very rare indeed when a thing like this happens to a country girl going to New York. She will have to do a good job next time if she goes on up. I feel what I think is a justifiable measure of pride in her accomplishment, and I must say she has displayed much determination, confidence and ambition to give up a good job in New York and take a chance at writing a book."[10]
>
> —AC Lee, after the publication of To Kill a Mockingbird

shy person, she was growing weary from all the attention. "Well, I can't say that [my reaction] was one of surprise," Lee said of her success in a radio interview following *Mockingbird*'s publication. "It was one of sheer numbness. It was like being hit over the head and knocked cold. . . . I hoped for a little, as I said, but I got rather a whole lot, and in some ways this was just about as frightening as the quick, merciful death I'd expected."[9] It was time for her to take a breather.

Back to Monroeville

Over the winter of 1960, Lee spent most of her time out of the prying eyes of the public. She visited her aging father, AC, who was now 81 years old and frail. She played golf and went on a few hunting excursions with friends. And she caught up on years of books she

Lee remained close to her father even after moving to New York City.

had always intended to read but never had the time for because of strict writing deadlines.

Lee's older sister Alice managed her business affairs and some of the details of *To Kill a Mockingbird*'s success. Fielding interview requests, answering fan mail, turning strangers away who came to the Lees' door hoping for an autograph—these were tasks Alice now handled to relieve her sister of some of the stress often associated with sudden fame. With her calm demeanor, sharp mind, and work in their father's law firm, Alice was more than happy to oblige.

But despite her disappearing act, Lee had not become a total recluse. She did grant an interview from time to time if the circumstances seemed significant enough. And in certain situations, like her reply to a request for background information from Huntingdon College, she never passed up an opportunity to take her just-beneath-the-surface sense of humor out for a spin. She responded in a letter to Huntingdon College:

> I'm afraid a biographical sketch of me will be sketchy indeed; With the exception of M'bird, nothing of any particular interest to anyone has happened to me in my thirty-four years. I was exposed to seventeen years of formal education in Monroeville schools, Huntingdon College, and the University of Alabama. If I ever learned anything, I've forgotten it.[11]

As for "M'bird," sales were still steady and strong by the end of its first year on the market. It had sold more than 2.5 million copies.[12] It was in the process of being translated into a slew of different languages, including French, German, Italian, Spanish, and Dutch. There were rumors that a movie studio in Hollywood was turning it into a film to be released sometime in 1962. And it had claimed a prestigious award not even the great Capote had managed to win: the Pulitzer Prize.

Lee had truly passed a milestone in her career. "I am as lucky as I can be," Lee told the *Birmingham News* after the Pulitzer win. "I don't know anyone who has been luckier."[14]

AWARD WINNER

In 1961, Harper Lee won the Pulitzer Prize—an award given in the United States each year for excellent work in writing, reporting, or music composition. That same year, *To Kill a Mockingbird* was also a finalist for another prestigious honor, the National Book Award. Since judges began doling out National Book Award designations in 1950, a number of novelists, poets, and nonfiction writers have won, including, in recent years, young adult authors such as Jacqueline Woodson, Cynthia Kadohata, and William Alexander.

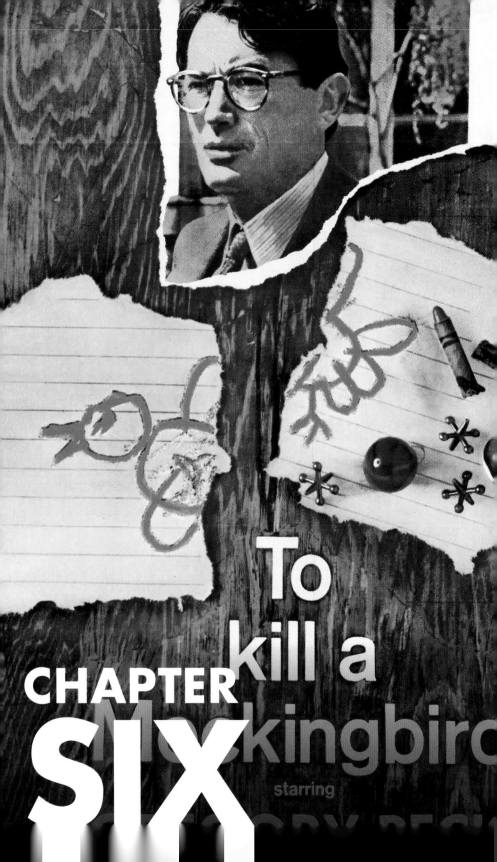

CHAPTER SIX

To kill a Mockingbird

starring

LIGHTS, CAMERA, ACTION

A few months prior to the Pulitzer win in the spring of 1961, Lee could officially boast another piece of excellent news. The rumors had been confirmed—film agent Annie Laurie Williams, Crain's wife, had sold the rights for *To Kill a Mockingbird* in February to filmmakers Robert Mulligan and Alan Pakula. Though the director and producer team still had not picked up distribution rights from Universal Studios, the book was on its way to being transformed into a major motion picture.

A new screenplay would have to be written, using dialogue from the book and adding more action to fill each scene. A filming location would have to be chosen. Could the small town of Monroeville, Alabama—surely the model of the book's small town—handle an influx of actors, film crew, and camera equipment? And of

Universal Studios planned to release a movie version of *To Kill a Mockingbird* in 1962.

course, the actors would have to be cast—who would play Atticus? Scout? Boo Radley?

There was a lot to be done in the two years it would take to make the movie, and all of it would have to fit within the film's modest estimated budget of $2 million.[1] That, and it would have to be approved by Lee and her family.

Building the Set

When producer Pakula traveled to Monroeville in February 1961 to scout out possible filming locations, he found a town rattled by change. Though separate water fountains marked "White" and "Colored" were still commonplace, gone were the African-American shacks that had been scattered throughout town during the early 1930s. Dusty dirt roads had been paved over with asphalt. Mailboxes and lampposts now lined the streets. New stores and cafés populated the modernized town square. The only building that remained relatively untouched was the brick Monroe County Courthouse.

Pakula and Mulligan felt Monroeville had been updated too much from when *To Kill a Mockingbird* was set to use the town as the setting for the movie.

Even the Lee family had moved into a brick ranch house across from the elementary school. The house where Truman once lived had been torn down, with nothing but a patch of grass left in its place. Only the stone wall between the two friends' houses remained intact.

After much deliberation, Pakula and Mulligan came up with a plan. It would be impossible to shoot a movie

Mulligan, along with Pakula, wanted to ensure the movie set accurately portrayed the 1930s and other details in the book.

in the current version of Monroeville. So in order to capture the true feel of 1932 Alabama, an entirely new set would have to be constructed on one of Hollywood's filming lots. Following Pakula's lead, art director Henry Bumstead traveled to Monroeville and interviewed the

Lees and other Monroeville natives about what their town looked like back then, poured through countless newspaper clippings and historical records, took measurements, and soaked up every last detail about the town and its inhabitants so he could faithfully create a set that mirrored what had been reality.

When the research was completed, Bumstead returned to Hollywood to begin construction. For the price of one dollar each, Universal Studios purchased a block of houses that had been scheduled for demolition. With a touch of paint, a dash of old charm, and a little refurbishing to add porches and porch swings, Bumstead turned the houses into models of those described in *To Kill a Mockingbird*. He also created an exact replica of the inside of the Monroe County Courthouse on a nearby soundstage to represent the courtroom where Atticus's legendary defense of Tom Robinson took place.

"If the integrity of a film adaptation is measured by the degree to which the novelist's intent is preserved, Mr. Foote's screenplay should be studied as a classic."[2]

—*Harper Lee*

Casting Actors

With the physical creation of Maycomb under way and a version of the book being adapted into a script by little-known screenwriter Horton Foote (Lee was given first dibs but declined), Mulligan and Pakula set about the task of hiring actors. Universal Studios had their own ideas about who might be perfect for the role of Atticus Finch. Well-known actor Spencer Tracy was one; Rock Hudson was another. In the end, a dark-haired, handsome, and gallant actor named Gregory Peck was offered the part, and he accepted.

"I got started on it and of course I sat up all night and read straight through it," Peck said when he received a copy of *To Kill a Mockingbird*. "I understood that they wanted me to play Atticus and I called them at about eight o'clock in the morning and said, 'If you want me to play Atticus, when do I start? I'd love to play it.'"[3]

In order to prepare for the role, Peck journeyed to Monroeville in January 1962 with his wife to get a feel for the town and do a character study of AC, the man widely believed to be the inspiration for Atticus. As soon as Lee took Peck on a personal tour with a stop at the Wee Diner for lunch, word got out. Admirers seeking autographs and women offering Peck and his wife southern baked goods mobbed Peck from that point forward.

Casting Peck in the role of Atticus Finch was relatively easy. A recommendation from Foote helped secure a then-unknown Robert Duvall for Boo Radley. And though Brock Peters had mostly played villains in the past, choosing him for the part of Tom Robinson also went smoothly. But finding children to capture the true essence of Scout, Jem, and Dill? Now that was a different story.

Though nine-year-old John Megna, a semi-seasoned actor who had already done a show on Broadway, played Dill, both nine-year-old Mary Badham and 13-year-old Phillip Alford were unknowns. In an open casting call in Birmingham, Alabama, just weeks before filming was scheduled to begin, the pair—who coincidentally

MARY BADHAM

Mary Badham adored playing the part of Scout. She loved the experience of being on set so much that on the last day of filming, she purposefully flubbed her lines over and over again so she would be able to do one more take. The nine-year-old Badham became the youngest girl (at the time) to receive an Oscar nomination for Best Supporting Actress. That year, the award went to Patty Duke, who played the part of Helen Keller in the 1962 film *The Miracle Worker*.

lived four blocks apart in Birmingham—were picked out of a crowd of kids hoping to nab a part in their first Hollywood movie. Alford, who was cast as Jem, only went to the audition because his parents promised him a day off from school. Badham, with her bowl-cut hairdo and piercing stare, has since shared in an interview that one of the reasons she secured the role was because of a

"GOOF" TRIVIA

In 2006, the film adaptation of *To Kill a Mockingbird* was ranked number 2 in the American Film Institute's 100 Most Inspiring Movies of All Time. There are a lot of little-known "goofs" that happened during its filming:

- The pennies in the cigar box in the beginning of the film are dated 1962, even though the film takes place in 1932.

- The first three numbers on the license plate on Atticus Finch's car change during the movie, from 709 to 358.

- When Scout and Jem are discussing whether Jem should go back to get his trousers from Boo Radley's, it is clear that Scout is mouthing Jem's lines.

- After returning from their visit to the Robinsons', Atticus carries the sleeping Scout down the hall to her bedroom. The error happens when he drops her off in the last room on the left; that is Jem's room!

- At the beginning of the film, Scout says, "Maycomb was a tired, old town, even in 1932 when I first knew it . . . Maycomb County had recently been told that it had nothing to fear but fear itself." This is in reference to President Franklin D. Roosevelt's inaugural address. But Roosevelt did not give that speech until 1933.[4]

snide retort she made to a talent scout who implied she was small for her age. "You'd be little, too, if you drank as much coffee as I do," she said.[5]

Months of Filming

After the kids had received their scripts, and with all the components in place, the business of filming *To Kill a Mockingbird* began and lasted for many months. Though the adults knew what they were doing for the most part, it took a bit of adjustment for the kids to stop horsing around and get into their respective roles. Lee even popped by the set in February 1962 to witness the story she had imagined all those years ago being brought so vividly to life:

> There seemed to be such a general kindness, perhaps even respect, for the material they were working with. I was delighted, touched, happy, and exceedingly grateful. I think this kindness and respect permeated everyone who had anything to do with the film, from the producer and the director down to the man who designed the sets, from Greg Peck to the peripheral characters, the actors who played the smaller parts.[6]

Watching as Peck expertly tapped into the spirit of Atticus and, indirectly, her father was especially rewarding for Lee. "The first glimpse I had of [Peck] was

Lee visited the *To Kill a Mockingbird* set to see how
the actors portrayed her famous characters.

when he came out of his dressing room in his Atticus suit. It was the most amazing transformation I had ever seen. . . . The minute I saw him I knew everything was going to be all right because he *was* Atticus."[7]

Unfortunately, the exhilaration Lee felt in Hollywood was short-lived. Just weeks after she returned to Monroeville from her visit, her father passed away. It was Palm Sunday—April 15, 1962. AC was 82 years old. An obituary that ran in the *Montgomery Advertiser* a week later stated, "What makes Atticus Finch or Amasa Coleman Lee, thus a remarkable man? He was a teacher of his own children, a small-town citizen who thought about things and tried to be a decent Christian human being. He succeeded."[8]

"*To Kill a Mockingbird* is about bigotry . . . For me the most beautiful scene is the moment when the Judge drops by to ask Atticus to take the case in defense of Tom Robinson. Casually put and casually answered, the question needed no answer. The judge knew it would not be possible for Atticus to say no. As for Jem and Scout, they learn a sense of honor from Atticus."[9]

—Gregory Peck

CHAPTER
SEVEN

NEEDING PRIVACY

Beginning in Hollywood on Christmas 1962, and stretching for months into 1963, *To Kill a Mockingbird* premiered in cinemas across the country. Lines wrapped around the block as eager moviegoers in cities such as New York City; Los Angeles, California; Detroit, Michigan; and Chicago, Illinois, scrambled to watch Peck become Atticus Finch in the film adaptation of Lee's Pulitzer Prize–winning novel. Many showings sold out the minute tickets went on sale, especially those in Monroeville and Birmingham.

The media lauded the film. Some said it was a slam dunk, echoing the opinion of Larry Tubelle from *Variety*, who wrote it was "a major film achievement, a significant, captivating and memorable picture that ranks with the best of recent years."[1] Others, such as Bosley Crowther from the *New York Times*, mostly enjoyed what they saw, but felt the balance between civil rights commentary and childlike perspective was slightly off. "There is so much feeling for children in the film . . .

Actor Gregory Peck attends the much-anticipated premiere of *To Kill a Mockingbird* in London, England.

it comes as a bit of a letdown at the end to realize that, for all the picture's feeling for children, it doesn't tell us very much of how they feel."[2]

Despite these critiques, Pakula and Mulligan's *To Kill a Mockingbird* was deemed a huge success. Of the eight Academy Awards nominations it received, including Best Picture, Best Supporting Actress (Mary Badham), and Best Director, the film won three of them—Best Adapted Screenplay (Horton Foote), Best Art/Set Direction (Henry Bumstead), and Best Actor (Gregory Peck). Watching the ceremony from a friend's house in Monroeville, Lee had every reason to be proud of the film's accomplishments. But that did not mean she would go out celebrating.

Fame Takes Its Toll

As publicity generated from the film's release began to wind down, Lee had had enough attention. Though her sister Alice was still handling the majority of her dealings with

LIVE MOCKINGBIRD WINS $10!

When the film premiered in Monroeville in late March 1963, the *Monroe Journal* ran a full-page ad and tickets went on sale weeks in advance—one dollar for adults and fifty cents for children. The first five moviegoers who brought in a live mockingbird received ten dollars in exchange as a prize.

the public, Lee continued to receive too many calls and too many letters. She was tired of being in the limelight and hunted down by the media for a quote about the book or an opinion about the movie. "Success has had a very bad effect on me," she mentioned to a reporter from the *Associated Press* in March 1963. "I've gotten fat—but extremely uncomplacent. I'm running just as scared as before."[3]

"In the book I tried to give a sense of proportion to life in the South, that there isn't a lynching before every breakfast. I think that Southerners react with the same kind of horror as other people do about the injustice in their land. In Mississippi, people were so revolted by what happened, they were so stunned, I don't think it will happen again."[5]
—*Lee in a press conference in Chicago shortly after the movie's release*

Normally a respite from the gritty, bustling streets of New York City, even Monroeville presented its own barriers to privacy. "I've found I can't write on my home grounds," Lee told a journalist from the *Cleveland Plain Dealer* on March 17, 1964. "I have about 300 personal friends who keep dropping in for a cup of coffee. I've tried getting up at 6, but then all the 6 o'clock risers congregate."[4]

So in the spring of 1964, Lee stopped granting interviews. With a few exceptions, including an

Lee, who was a private person, was not used to all of the attention she would receive in the years following the release of her book or its movie.

extensive conversation with *Counterpoint* host Roy Newquist on WQXR radio and an article for *TIME*, she declined any further effort to promote herself or *To Kill a Mockingbird*. "As time went on she said that reporters began to take too many liberties with what she said," recalled Alice in the documentary *Hey Boo: Harper Lee and To Kill a Mockingbird*. "So she just wanted out . . . She felt like she'd given enough."[6]

With a renewed sense of purpose for a new project, Lee returned to her apartment on the Upper East Side of Manhattan. In a city with hundreds of thousands of people, she could be more anonymous than in her small childhood town. She would have access to the home of her agents, Williams and Crain, in the Connecticut countryside if she needed peace and quiet. And the demand for a follow-up novel was so great that she wanted to get back to the business of writing again.

AN INVITATION TO THE WHITE HOUSE

In 1966, President Lyndon B. Johnson appointed Lee to the National Council of the Arts. With the appointment came an invitation to the White House. By that time, Lee had stopped speaking to the press. Sources close to the author said she did not dress up for the occasion, but she did accept the honor, which came with a six-year term.

Lee was also anxious to reunite with Capote. Since her rise to fame and the success of the movie, Capote had grown distant. He was hard at work putting the finishing touches on *In Cold Blood*, and though she willingly took time off from matters involving *To Kill a Mockingbird* to travel back to Kansas a few times for

DID CAPOTE WRITE *TO KILL A MOCKINGBIRD*?

Capote was a prolific writer, publishing novels, screenplays, many essays and short stories. It is for that reason that a persistent rumor has followed Lee when it became apparent that a second book was not coming—that her childhood friend actually wrote *To Kill a Mockingbird*. Lee insists this is false. Some theorists claim Capote was such a literary genius that he adopted Lee's voice and wrote the novel for her when it became apparent she was struggling. Others insist he stepped in at the end and edited her efforts to reflect more of what he had in mind. And though Capote never said

he wrote Lee's book, he never explicitly denied it either. But in 2006, a letter from Capote to his aunt, dated July 9, 1959, resurfaced. "It says that a year before the novel was published in July of 1960, [Capote] had seen the novel, had read much of the book, and liked it very much, and commented that she has great talent," said Wayne Flynt, a retired professor of history at Auburn University, in an interview with NPR. "I don't know that we needed this letter, but I suppose it does put to rest some of the naysayers out there and some of the people who have claimed that she really is not a great literary talent."[7]

last-minute research to help him, Capote was not as accommodating of her as he had been a few years earlier.

Some close to the pair suspected Capote's bruised ego had gotten in the way of their friendship. Although his career had blossomed much earlier than Lee's, the fame he achieved had taken much longer and had involved many more years of hardship than Lee endured. Plus, Lee had won a Pulitzer. Capote had been chasing the prize for years and still had not won.

Capote Makes a Splash

In the end, Capote would never win the Pulitzer. He did not win the National Book Award either. But when *In Cold Blood* was first serialized in the *New Yorker* magazine on September 25, 1965, and then released in hardcover in January 1966, sales of the book went through the roof. Capote became even more of an attention-crazed celebrity and lapped up his resurgent fame—staying out at all hours, drinking, partying, and doing a lot of drugs.

And Lee? When she opened her copy of *In Cold Blood* for the first time, she was shocked to discover Capote had merely dedicated the book to her. Nowhere on the rest of the pages was there any mention of

Lee's contribution. The research she had done and the interviews she had slogged through. The meticulous edits and unconditional support she had given Capote. Nothing. To the unsuspecting eye, Lee and the people mentioned in the book could have been strangers. "Nelle was very hurt that she didn't get more credit because she wrote half that book," recalled Lee's friend R. Philip Hanes.[8]

Though Lee never went public with her feelings about her strained relationship with Capote or about his slow but steady descent into a debauched lifestyle that would soon get the better of him, it is believed she and Capote fell out of touch in subsequent years and stayed that way. When Capote later died at age 59 in 1984 of liver failure—balding, paunchy, and with an unfinished novel called *Answered Prayers* that had been dogging him for more than a decade—some suspected his childhood best friend had not spoken to him in years.

Frustration and Loss

By the time 1970 rolled around, there was only one question on everyone's mind when it came to the subject of Lee: When would her next book be published? In fact, Lee was asking herself the same question. She had been

Lee mentioned to her close friends she was upset by the lack of credit she was given for helping Capote with *In Cold Blood*.

wrestling with a second manuscript—another story supposedly set in the South—that had not yet come to fruition:

> I would like, however, to do one thing, and I've never spoken much about it because it's such a personal thing. I would like to leave some record of the kind of life that existed in a very small world. I hope to do this in several novels—to chronicle something that seems to be very quickly going down the drain. This is small-town middle-class southern life as opposed to the Gothic, as opposed to Tobacco Road, as opposed to plantation life . . . In other words all I want to be is the Jane Austen of south Alabama.[9]

GO SET A WATCHMAN FOUND!

In February 2015, the literary world woke up to astounding news. *Go Set a Watchman*, the novel Lee wrote before *To Kill a Mockingbird*, had been found! Soon after the missing manuscript was discovered in late 2014 by Lee's lawyer Tonja Carter, Lee's publisher HarperCollins announced the book would be released on July 14, 2015, with an initial print run of 2 million copies.[10]

"I hadn't realized it had survived, so was surprised and delighted when my dear friend and lawyer Tonja Carter discovered it. After much thought and hesitation I shared it with a handful of people I trust and was pleased to hear that they considered it worthy of publication. I am humbled and amazed that this will now be published after all these years," Lee said in a written statement.[11]

Then, in April 1970, the first of a series of blows blocked Lee's progress even further. Her longtime friend and agent, Crain, died of cancer, and his wife, Williams, closed their business, retaining only a few key clients. Soon after, Lee's editor Hohoff retired from J. B. Lippincott and died in 1974. Lee never admitted as much, but perhaps it was the loss of the people who helped shape *To Kill a Mockingbird* into the masterpiece it became that prevented Lee from going public about the status of her original novel, *Go Set a Watchman*. Maybe it is also the reason why Lee never finished another project she started in the 1980s called *The Reverend*, a true-crime novel loosely based on the trial of an African-American

After decades of thinking her original manuscript, *Go Set a Watchman*, was lost, Lee was reportedly happy about its 2015 release.

preacher named W. M. Maxwell and the mysterious circumstances surrounding the deaths of five of his relatives. That, or she just wanted to stop while she was ahead.

CHAPTER
EIGHT

HARPER LEE'S LEGACY

O n April 28, 2015, Nelle Harper Lee turned 89 years old. Though Alice died on November 17, 2014, at 103, she had continued to practice law until the ripe old age of 100. Neither woman ever married. Both ended up in a Monroeville assisted-living facility. But the two sisters enjoyed long and fruitful lives and made a noteworthy imprint on the world.

Since the turn of the millennium, Lee has continued to weather the highs and lows that have accompanied her success. In 2001, she was inducted into the Alabama Academy of Honor, a distinction awarded to important people born or living in the state.

In conjunction with the ceremony, the Honors College at the University of Alabama sponsored its first essay contest on the merits of *To Kill a Mockingbird*, open to all high school students in Alabama. Until her move

Even though *To Kill a Mockingbird* is more than 50 years old, Lee continues to be awarded and praised for her work and contribution to the literary world.

into the nursing home, Lee attended the ceremony every year to congratulate the contest's winners. "What these people have done for me is wonderful," she told a reporter for the *New York Times* in a rare 2006 interview. "They always see new things in [*To Kill a Mockingbird*]. The way they relate it to their lives now is really quite incredible."[1]

On November 5, 2007, President George W. Bush presented Lee with the highest civilian honor in the United States, the Presidential Medal of Freedom, for her "outstanding contribution to America's literary tradition."[2] Just before the president slipped the medal over Lee's head, the ceremony's moderator announced, "Harper Lee's beautiful book is a meditation on family, human complexity, and some of the great themes of American life. At a critical moment in our history, *To Kill a Mockingbird* helped focus the nation on the turbulent struggle for equality."[3]

"The messages [of *To Kill a Mockingbird*] are so clear and so simple. It's a way of life and thinking about life and getting along with one another and learning tolerance. Racism and bigotry haven't gone anywhere. Ignorance hasn't gone anywhere. This is not a black and white 1930s America issue. These are issues that are global."[4]
—Mary Badham, the actress who played Scout in the 1962 movie adaptation

The Presidential Medal of Freedom is the highest civilian award given out each year. Lee received her award in 2007.

Three and a half years later, President Barack Obama followed up the honor and awarded Lee with the 2010 National Medal of Arts, though she was not able to attend the White House celebration because of her frailty. "The National Medal of Arts recipients represent the many vibrant and diverse art forms thriving in America," said National Endowment for the Arts Chairman Rocco Landesman.[5]

Lee has aged in the last decade, suffering a stroke and losing some of her eyesight and hearing. But her old age certainly has not lessened the impact of *To Kill a Mockingbird*. And with the publication of *Go Set a Watchman* in 2015, readers will now be able to find out what happens to Scout, Atticus, and Boo Radley 20 years after the action of *Mockingbird* takes place.

Controversy Bubbles Over

July 2010 marked the fiftieth anniversary of *To Kill a Mockingbird*'s publication. In commemoration, the people

A HIT AMONG READERS

Since its publication, *To Kill a Mockingbird* has been taught in classrooms and is a mainstay in public libraries around the world. In August 2001, Chicago launched an initiative to get every adult in the city to read Lee's book at the same time. As part of the One Book, One Chicago campaign, participants were given pins adorned with mockingbirds to help spot fellow readers around town. More than 6,500 library patrons participated, 350 of whom used copies that had been translated into a foreign language.[6] Discussions and film screenings were held throughout the city.

In 2009, *To Kill a Mockingbird* was chosen for the National Endowment for the Arts The Big Read campaign, a program launched in 2006 to unite communities across the United States through books and reading. Grants are given to organizations that wish to participate, and "the read" lasts for one month. In addition to these initiatives, *To Kill a Mockingbird* has been a top pick for hundreds of other educational programs for both children and adults, promoting tolerance and literacy in cities and schools nationwide.

of Monroeville staged a giant celebratory festival for hundreds of tourists, a small portion of the thousands who flock to the small town every year to catch a glimpse of the spot that inspired *Mockingbird*'s Maycomb and the birthplace of one of the greatest authors in US history. There were cook-offs featuring typical southern fare and Lee documentary screenings. Tours of local landmarks included a stop at Mel's Dairy Dream (where Lee's childhood home once stood) and the Monroe County Courthouse (fully restored and now a museum).

But since that milestone weekend, unfortunately, a number of controversies have popped up that threaten to mar Lee's virtually untarnished reputation. In 2001, a writer named Marja Mills traveled to Monroeville to write a story on the town for the *Chicago Tribune*. Three years later, she rented a house next door to the Lees in order to research a book she planned to write about what she referred to as their blossoming friendship. Mills insisted her book was written with the full cooperation of Lee. But when *The Mockingbird Next Door: Life with Harper Lee* was published in July 2014, almost exactly 54 years to the day after *To Kill a Mockingbird*'s release, Lee insisted she had nothing to do with it.

Mills's book quickly became a source of
controversy after it was published.

"It did not take long to discover Marja's true mission; another book about Harper Lee. I was hurt, angry and saddened, but not surprised. I immediately cut off all contact with Miss Mills, leaving town whenever she headed this way," Lee wrote in a statement issued on July 14, 2014. "Rest assured, as long as I am alive any book purporting to be with my cooperation is a falsehood."[7] The truth of the matter has yet to be determined.

Meanwhile, Lee had become entangled in two different lawsuits—the first was in May 2013 against Samuel Pinkus, the son-in-law of the agent who inherited Lee as a client after her first agent, Crain, passed away. In 2007, Pinkus had sent the frail, then 80-year-old Lee a letter. In it, he asked that she hand over the copyright of *To Kill a Mockingbird* to him, thereby entitling him to a portion of the royalties—money from future sales of the book. Having just suffered a stroke, Lee reportedly

"This is a memoir, I should say, and not a biography, so this does not examine every part of her life beginning to end. It's really more a chance for readers to have this extraordinary experience, which was what it felt like to sit at the kitchen table having coffee with Nelle Harper and talking about Truman Capote and literature . . . This is the book that [she and Alice] very much helped me shape . . . I just know that it's true to the spirit of the time I spent with them."[8]
—Marja Mills in an interview on National Public Radio after her book was published in 2014

signed the document without fully understanding what it entailed. Though Lee successfully regained control of the copyright, the full extent of the circumstances surrounding Pinkus's vast web of deception has yet to be uncovered.

In August 2013, Lee filed suit against the Monroe County Museum with the help of Tonja Carter, a cousin of Capote's and a partner in Alice's law firm who took over Lee's affairs after Alice retired. Under the terms of the lawsuit, Lee was suing the museum for its "exploitation" of her novel for the purpose of merchandizing *Mockingbird*-branded T-shirts, mugs, and other such memorabilia. Though the museum eventually settled out of court, some people, such as Sam Therrell, who owns Radley's Fountain Grill in Monroeville, suggest Carter might have initiated the lawsuit without Lee's full consent. "I don't think Miss Nelle or Alice had anything to do with it," he told a reporter. "It's her agent and her local lawyer. I don't know what kind of relationship they entered into, how she ever became of counsel . . . [but] it was stupid to let it happen, I can tell you that."[9]

Tourists could buy aprons, coasters, and cookbooks with *Mockingbird* branding before Lee sued the Monroe County Museum in 2013.

A Lasting Impact

For a person who shunned media coverage, Lee has certainly attracted her fair share late in life. But despite the lawsuits and controversies, there is no question her legacy remains fully intact. As of 2015, *To Kill a Mockingbird* has sold more than 40 million copies worldwide since it has been in print. It has been translated into 40 different languages and counting.[10] It is taught in middle school and high school classrooms

DID LEE REALLY GIVE HER CONSENT?

When HarperCollins leaked the news that *Go Set a Watchman* had been "discovered" by Lee's lawyer Carter after Alice's death, many people in the publishing community and the public at large were skeptical about whether the publicity-shy Lee actually gave her consent. Some old friends in Monroeville insist Lee is too infirm to have willingly consented to *Watchman*'s release. Others suggest it is a publicity stunt by Lee's current agent and publisher, hoping to cash in on a celebrated author's legacy.

Michael Morrison, the president and publisher of HarperCollins, and Jonathan Burnham, the senior vice president and publisher of Harper, both deny such is the case. "She was in great spirits, and we talked about how much we love 'Go Set a Watchman' and the details of the publication," Morrison said in a statement to the *Times* after he and Burnham visited Lee at the nursing home in February 2015. "It was a great meeting, and as expected, she was humorous, intelligent and gracious."[11]

around the world. And it sells more than 1 million copies each year.[12]

Perhaps 2013 National Book Award winner James McBride put it best when he said *To Kill a Mockingbird* "speaks to the general problem of four hundred years of racism, slavery, socio-economic classism . . . the courage of the working class, the isolation of the South, the identity crisis of a young girl, and the coming out of a neighborhood recluse."[13] Without a doubt, the book remains one of the most popular books of all time.

So, too, Lee can be viewed as a model and inspiration for any aspiring writer. In a telling quote from one of her last full live interviews in 1964, she offered a few words of advice:

> Hope for the best and expect nothing. Then you won't be disappointed. . . . People who write for reward by way of recognition or monetary gain don't know what they're doing. They're in the category of those who write; they are not writers. Writing is simply something you must do. It's rather like virtue in that it is its own reward.[14]

As of May 2015, *To Kill a Mockingbird* was still one of the top-selling novels of all time. Fifty-five years after *Mockingbird* was originally published, its "parent" novel, *Go Set a Watchman*, was following in its footsteps.

> "Real courage [is] when you know you're licked before you begin but you begin anyway and you see it through no matter what. You rarely win, but sometimes you do."[16]
>
> —*Atticus Finch*

Watchman topped preorder best seller lists, including Amazon.com before its release. And foreign rights had been sold in at least 25 territories.[15] While Lee did not do a nationwide tour because of her failing health, there is no doubt *Watchman*'s publication made a memorable impact on minds young and old the world over. How will critics and the public react as this new chapter in Lee's legacy unfolds? Only time will tell.

Many readers were excited to read Lee's highly anticipated novel *Go Set a Watchman* and learn more about their favorite *Mockingbird* characters.

TIMELINE

1926
Nelle Harper Lee is born on April 28 in Monroeville, Alabama.

1930
Truman Streckfus Persons (i.e., Truman Capote) moves in next door to the Lees.

1944
Lee attends Huntingdon College.

1945
Lee transfers to the University of Alabama to study law and write for the *Rammer Jammer*.

1949
Lee moves to New York City and gets a job as an airplane reservations agent.

1956

Michael and Joy Brown give Lee a large sum of
money for Christmas so she can take a year off
and write; Lee begins work on her first novel.

1957

Lee submits the first draft of her manuscript for *To Kill a
Mockingbird* to J. B. Lippincott; Lippincott offers her a
contract, with the prerequisite that she rewrite the novel.

1959

Lee accompanies Capote to Holcomb,
Kansas, to help research a story he is writing
about the murder of the Clutter family.

1960

To Kill a Mockingbird is published on July 11,
with an initial print run of 5,000 copies. The
book becomes an immediate success, and a
second and third printing are swiftly ordered.

1961

Lee wins the Pulitzer Prize for Best American Novel;
she is a finalist for the National Book Award; film
rights for the book are sold to Universal Studios.

TIMELINE

1962
The film *To Kill a Mockingbird* opens on December 25. Audiences and critics alike adore the film.

1964
Lee gives one of her last in-depth media interviews to Roy Newquist for his radio show, *Counterpoint*. The conversation is later included in a book of the same name.

1966
President Lyndon B. Johnson appoints Lee to the National Council of the Arts. She accepts.

2001
Lee is inducted into the Alabama Academy of Honor; the University of Alabama holds its first annual *To Kill a Mockingbird* essay contest for high school students across the state. Lee attends every year until her stroke in 2007.

2007

President George W. Bush presents Lee
with the Presidential Medal of Freedom at
the White House on November 5.

2011

President Barack Obama awards Lee the
National Medal of Arts on March 2.

2013

Lee becomes involved in two lawsuits regarding
the copyright of *To Kill a Mockingbird* and
the exploitation of its trademark.

2014

Marja Mills publishes *The Mockingbird Next Door*, a
book to which Lee insists she didn't give consent.

2015

Go Set a Watchman is published on July 14.

ESSENTIAL FACTS

Date of Birth
April 28, 1926

Place of Birth
Monroeville, Alabama

Parents
Amasa Coleman and Frances Cunningham Finch Lee

Education
Monroe County High School
Huntingdon College
University of Alabama
University of Oxford

Career Highlights
Lee's *To Kill a Mockingbird* is still one of the most widely read novels by both children and adults more than 50 years after it was first published. In 1961, it won the prestigious Pulitzer Prize in Fiction and has sold more than 30 million copies worldwide, been translated into more than 40 languages, and sells more than 1 million copies each year. In 2001, Lee was inducted into the Alabama Academy of Honor. She received the Presidential Medal of Freedom for her contribution to literature in 2007, and the National Medal of Arts in 2010. Lee's earlier novel, *Go Set a Watchman*, which resurfaced in 2014, was published on July 14, 2015.

Societal Contribution

Though *To Kill a Mockingbird* takes place in the 1930s, it was published in 1960, just as the civil rights movement was unfolding in the United States. Not much had changed in the prejudiced and deeply segregated South, and Lee was one of the first white authors to accurately portray the struggles African Americans faced during that time in a book that advocated for compassion, equality, and freedom for all people.

Conflicts

Lee's close friends and family have always described her as a warm, thoughtful, and incredibly generous person. But over the years she has developed a reputation for being private and tight-lipped. She has not granted a media interview in more than 40 years and was involved in three different lawsuits, all while she was in her 80s. She sued the Monroe County Museum for improper use of her novel; her second agent's son-in-law, Samuel Pinkus, for copyright infringement; and author Marja Mills for writing an unauthorized memoir about her life. There are also rumors that she and Truman Capote had a falling-out.

Quote

"My needs are simple: paper, pen, and privacy."—*Harper Lee*

GLOSSARY

civil rights
The rights of citizens to political and social freedom and equality.

copyright
The exclusive legal right, given to an originator or an assignee, to print, publish, perform, film, or record literary, artistic, or musical material, and to authorize others to do the same.

distribution rights
A legal agreement that allows a person or company to sell a product in a particular area.

documentary
A book, movie, or television or radio program that provides a factual record or report.

editor
Someone who alters or revises another's work for publication.

Great Depression
The longest and most severe economic crash ever experienced by the Western world, stretching from 1929 to 1939.

Ku Klux Klan
An American post–Civil War society advocating white supremacy.

literary agent
Someone who acts on behalf of an author in dealing with publishers.

lynch
To kill someone, especially by hanging.

prejudice
A preconceived opinion that is based on matters of race, religion, sex, or sexual orientation.

Pulitzer Prize
An award for an achievement in US journalism, literature, or music; there are 14 given each year.

segregate
To separate people based on race, sex, religious beliefs, or other characteristics.

serialize
To publish or broadcast a story or play in regular installments.

soundstage
The part of a movie studio where a production is filmed.

ADDITIONAL RESOURCES

Selected Bibliography

Kachka, Boris. "The Decline of Harper Lee." *Vulture*. New York Media, 3 Feb. 2015. Web. 19 May 2015.

Mills, Marja. *The Mockingbird Next Door: Life with Harper Lee*. New York: Penguin, 2014. Print.

Palmer, R. Barton. *Harper Lee's To Kill a Mockingbird: The Relationship Between Text and Film*. London: Methuen Drama, 2008. Print.

Shields, Charles J. *Mockingbird: A Portrait of Harper Lee*. New York: Henry Holt, 2006. Print.

Further Readings

Don, Katherine. *Real Courage: The Story of Harper Lee*. Greensboro, NC: Morgan Reynolds, 2013. Print.

Lee, Harper. *To Kill a Mockingbird: 50th Anniversary Edition*. New York: HarperCollins, 2010. Print.

Websites

To learn more about Essential Lives, visit **booklinks.abdopublishing.com**. These links are routinely monitored and updated to provide the most current information available.

Places to Visit

Civil Rights Memorial and Center
400 Washington Avenue
Montgomery, AL 36104
334-956-8479
http://www.splcenter.org/civil-rights-memorial
This memorial contains the names of important figures
who died during the civil rights movement and chronicles
significant events that took place during that time.

Monroe County Museum
31 North Alabama Avenue
Monroeville, Alabama 36460
251-575-7433
http://www.monroecountymuseum.org
Restored to its original 1930s appearance, this iconic
Monroeville building is the model for the book's (and
movie's) courtroom scenes.

National Civil Rights Museum at the Lorraine Motel
450 Mulberry Street
Memphis, TN 38103
901-521-9699
http://civilrightsmuseum.org
Visitors walk through decades of civil rights history exhibits.

SOURCE NOTES

Chapter 1. Enough!
1. David L. Ulin. "Mixed Feelings on Harper Lee's 'Go Set a Watchman.'" *Los Angeles Times*. Tribune Media, 4 Feb. 2015. Web. 19 May 2015.
2. Harper Lee. *To Kill a Mockingbird: 50th Anniversary Edition*. New York: HarperCollins, 2010. Print. 36.
3. David McGee. "To Kill a Mockingbird Turns 50." *The Blue Grass Special*. The Blue Grass Special, 2009. Web. 19 May 2015.
4. Charles J. Shields. *Mockingbird: A Portrait of Harper Lee*. New York: Henry Holt, 2006. Print. 131.

Chapter 2. Monroeville
1. Sarah Lawless. "Monroeville." *Encyclopedia of Alabama*. Alabama Humanities Foundation, 18 Dec. 2012. Web. 19 May 2015.
2. Charles J. Shields. *Mockingbird: A Portrait of Harper Lee*. New York: Henry Holt, 2006. Print. 39.
3. Ibid. 34.
4. David McGee. "To Kill a Mockingbird Turns 50." *The Blue Grass Special*. The Blue Grass Special, 2009. Web. 19 May 2015.
5. George Thomas Jones. "Queen of the Tomboys." *Swisseduc.ch*. SwissEduc-Team, 31 May 2013. Web. 19 May 2015.

Chapter 3. A Writer Emerges
1. Charles J. Shields. *Mockingbird: A Portrait of Harper Lee*. New York: Henry Holt, 2006. Print. 77.
2. "Harper Lee." *Bio*. A&E Television Networks, 2015. Web. 19 May 2015.
3. Harper Lee. "Christmas to Me." *McCall's*. McCall Company, Dec. 1961. Web. 19 May 2015.

Chapter 4. *Atticus* Takes Shape
1. *Hey, Boo: Harper Lee and "To Kill a Mockingbird."* Dir. Mary McDonagh Murphy. Perf. Mary Badham, Rick Bragg, Alice Lee, Tom Brokaw, Oprah Winfrey. First Run Features, 2011. DVD.
2. Charles J. Shields. *Mockingbird: A Portrait of Harper Lee*. New York: Henry Holt, 2006. Print. 116.
3. Ibid. 118.
4. Ibid. 130.
5. Ibid. 133.
6. "Wealthy Farmer, 3 of Family Slain." *New York Times*. The New York Times Company, 16 Nov. 1959. Web. 19 May 2015.

7. "Scene of the Crime: Twenty-Five Years Later, Holcomb, Kansas Remembers 'In Cold Blood.'" *Chicago Sunday Tribune*. Tribune Publishing, 11 Nov. 1984. Web. 19 May 2015.

8. Charles J. Shields. *Mockingbird: A Portrait of Harper Lee*. New York: Henry Holt, 2006. Print. 157.

Chapter 5. *Mockingbird* Published

1. Ed. Gerald Clark. *Too Brief a Treat: The Letters of Truman Capote*. New York: Random, 2004. Print. 284.

2. David McGee. "To Kill a Mockingbird Turns 50." *The Blue Grass Special*. The Blue Grass Special, 2009. Web. 19 May 2015.

3. "To Kill a Mockingbird." *Pulitzer Prize First Edition Guide*. PPrize First Edition Guide, 2006. Web. 19 May 2015.

4. Richard Sullivan. "Early On It Was Recognized as a Novel of 'Rare Excellence.'" *Chicago Tribune*. The Chicago Tribune Company, 6 Aug. 2001. Web. 19 May 2015.

5. Frank H Lyell. "One-Taxi Town." *New York Times*. The New York Times, 10 Jul. 1960. Web. 19 May 2015.

6. "To Kill a Mockingbird." *The Big Read*. Arts Midwest, n.d. Web. 19 May 2015.

7. Ed. Gerald Clark. *Too Brief a Treat: The Letters of Truman Capote*. New York: Random, 2004. Print. 299.

8. *Hey, Boo: Harper Lee and "To Kill a Mockingbird."* Dir. Mary McDonagh Murphy. Perf. Mary Badham, Rick Bragg, Alice Lee, Tom Brokaw, Oprah Winfrey. First Run Features, 2011. DVD.

9. David McGee. "To Kill a Mockingbird Turns 50." *The Blue Grass Special*. The Blue Grass Special, 2009. Web. 19 May 2015.

10. Charles J. Shields. *Mockingbird: A Portrait of Harper Lee*. New York: Henry Holt, 2006. Print. 193.

11. Charles J. Shields. *I Am Scout: The Biography of Harper Lee*. New York: Henry Holt, 2008. Print. 133.

12. Charles J. Shields. *Mockingbird: A Portrait of Harper Lee*. New York: Henry Holt, 2006. Print. 202.

13. Boris Kachka. "The Decline of Harper Lee." *Vulture*. New York Media, 3 Feb. 2015. Web. 19 May 2015.

14. Alex Walsh. "Harper Lee on Winning Pulitzer in 1961: 'I Am as Lucky as I Can Be.'" *Al.com*. Alabama Media Group, 20 Mar. 2014. Web. 19 May 19, 2015.

Chapter 6. Lights, Camera, Action

1. "To Kill a Mockingbird." *IMDb*. IMDb.com, 2015. Web. 19 May 2015.

2. "To Kill a Mockingbird." *The Big Read*. Arts Midwest, n.d. Web. 19 May 2015.

SOURCE NOTES CONTINUED

3. Scott McGee, Kerryn Sherrod, and Jeff Stafford. "To Kill a Mockingbird (1962)." *TCM*. Turner Entertainment Networks, 2015. Web. 19 May 2015.

4. "To Kill a Mockingbird." *IMDb*. IMDb.com, 2015. Web. 19 May 2015.

5. Barbara Vancheri. "Author Lauded 'Mockingbird' as a 'Moving' Film." *Post-Gazette*. PG Publishing, 20 Feb. 2003. Web. 19 May 2015.

6. David McGee. "To Kill a Mockingbird Turns 50." *The Blue Grass Special*. The Blue Grass Special, 2009. Web. 19 May 2015.

7. Ibid.

8. Charles J. Shields. *Mockingbird: A Portrait of Harper Lee*. New York: Henry Holt, 2006. Print. 215.

9. "To Kill a Mockingbird." *The Big Read*. Arts Midwest, n.d. Web. 19 May 2015.

Chapter 7. Needing Privacy

1. Larry Tubelle. "Review: 'To Kill a Mockingbird.'" *Variety*. Variety Media, 11 Dec. 1962. Web. 19 May 2015.

2. Bosley Crowther. "To Kill a Mockingbird." *New York Times*. The New York Times Company, 15 Feb. 1963. Web. 19 May 2015.

3. Mary Murphy. "The No-Publicity Bestseller: On Harper Lee." *Publishers Weekly*. PWxyz, 28 June 2010. Web. 19 May 2015.

4. Charles J. Shields. *I Am Scout: The Biography of Harper Lee*. New York: Henry Holt, 2008. Print. 173.

5. Charles J. Shields. *Mockingbird: A Portrait of Harper Lee*. New York: Henry Holt, 2006. Print. 222.

6. *Hey, Boo: Harper Lee and "To Kill a Mockingbird."* Dir. Mary McDonagh Murphy. Perf. Mary Badham, Rick Bragg, Alice Lee, Tom Brokaw, Oprah Winfrey. First Run Features, 2011. DVD.

7. Melissa Block. "Letter Puts End to Persistent 'Mockingbird' Rumor." *NPR*. National Public Radio, 3 Mar. 2006. Web. 19 May 2015.

8. Charles J. Shields. *Mockingbird: A Portrait of Harper Lee*. New York: Henry Holt, 2006. Print. 253.

9. David McGee. "To Kill a Mockingbird Turns 50." *The Blue Grass Special*. The Blue Grass Special, 2009. Web. 19 May 2015.

10. Alison Flood and Paul Lewis. "Harper Lee to Publish New Novel, 55 Years After 'To Kill a Mockingbird.'" *Guardian*. Guardian News and Media, 3 Feb. 2015. Web. 19 May 2015.

11. Ibid.

Chapter 8. Harper Lee's Legacy

1. Ginia Bellafante. "Harper Lee, Gregarious for a Day." *New York Times*. The New York Times Company, 30 Jan. 2006. Web. 19 May 2015.

2. Kevin Howell "Harper Lee Wins Presidential Medal of Freedom." *Publishers Weekly.* PWxyz, 30 Oct. 2007. Web. 19 May 2015.

3. USA Patriotism! "2007 Presidential Medal of Freedom Ceremony." Online video clip. *YouTube.* YouTube, 19 Oct. 2011. Web. 19 May 2015.

4. *Hey, Boo: Harper Lee and "To Kill a Mockingbird."* Dir. Mary McDonagh Murphy. Perf. Mary Badham, Rick Bragg, Alice Lee, Tom Brokaw, Oprah Winfrey. First Run Features, 2011. DVD.

5. "White House Announces 2010 National Medal of Arts Recipients." *National Endowment for the Arts.* USA.gov, 1 Mar. 2011. Web. 19 May 2015.

6. "To Kill a Mockingbird." *The Big Read.* Arts Midwest, n.d. Web. 19 May 2015.

7. Lindsey Bahr. "Harper Lee Speaks: Marja Mills-Penned Bio Was Unauthorized (Updated)." *Entertainment Weekly.* Entertainment Weekly, 18 Jan. 2015. Web. 19 May 2015.

8. "To Meet A 'Mockingbird': Memoir Recalls Talks With Harper Lee." *NPR.* National Public Radio, 19 Jul. 2014. Web. 19 May 2015.

9. Boris Kachka. "The Decline of Harper Lee." *Vulture.* New York Media, 3 Feb. 2015. Web. 19 May 2015.

10. "HarperCollins to Publish Harper Lee's 'To Kill a Mockingbird' for the First Time as an E-Book and Digital Audio." *HarperCollins Publishers.* HarperCollins Publishers, 28 Apr. 2014. Web. 19 May 2015.

11. Serge F. Kovaleski, Alexandra Alter, and Jennifer Crossley Howard. "Harper Lee's Condition Debated by Friends, Fans and Now State of Alabama." *New York Times.* The New York Times Company, 11 Mar. 2015. Web. 19 May 2015.

12. "HarperCollins to Publish Harper Lee's 'To Kill a Mockingbird' for the First Time as an E-Book and Digital Audio." *HarperCollins Publishers.* HarperCollins Publishers, 28 Apr. 2014. Web. 19 May 2015.

13. *Hey, Boo: Harper Lee and "To Kill a Mockingbird."* Dir. Mary McDonagh Murphy. Perf. Mary Badham, Rick Bragg, Alice Lee, Tom Brokaw, Oprah Winfrey. First Run Features, 2011. DVD.

14. David McGee. "To Kill a Mockingbird Turns 50." *The Blue Grass Special.* The Blue Grass Special, 2009. Web. 19 May 2015.

15. Isabella Biedenharn. "Harper Lee's 'Go Set a Watchman' Attracts Interest from Foreign Publishers." *Entertainment Weekly.* Entertainment Weekly, 14 Apr. 2015. Web. 19 May 2015.

16. Harper Lee. *To Kill a Mockingbird: 50th Anniversary Edition.* New York: HarperCollins, 2010. Print. 149.

INDEX

ABOUT THE AUTHOR

Alexis Burling has written dozens of articles and books for young readers on a variety of topics including current events and famous people, nutrition and fitness, careers and money management, relationships, and cooking. She is also a book critic (and obsessive reader!) with reviews of both adult and young adult books, author interviews, and other industry-related articles published in the *New York Times*, *Washington Post*, *Chicago Tribune*, and more. Alexis remembers reading—and adoring—*To Kill a Mockingbird* when she was in middle school. She was inspired by Scout's confidence and spunk and loved Atticus because he reminded her of her own father.